The Mysteries of the Rosary

The Mysteries of the Rosary

Poems by

Martin Achatz

Mayapple Press 2004

© Copyright 2004 by Martin Achatz

Published by   MAYAPPLE PRESS
408 N. Lincoln St.
Bay City, MI 48708
www.mayapplepress.com

ISBN 0-932412-28-9

Acknowledgements:

Some of these poems first appeared in the following publications:
Kenesaw Review—"Sleeping with Grief" and "Evolution"
Paterson Literary Review—"Place in the Forest"

The author would like to thank Dr. Beverly Matherne for her unflagging friendship, encouragement, and faith; Dr. Austin Hummell for his keen eye and tremendous support; Dr. Diane Sautter for her good karma; his family for all the love; the staff of the Upper Peninsula Surgery Center for its undying patience; and Beth, for all the joy, sorrow, light, and glory.

Cover art by Matthew Dryer.

Cover and book design by Judith Kerman; typeset by Judith Kerman in Callisto MT text with ITC Avant Garde titles.

Contents

The Mysteries of the Rosary   7

Prayer   9
Simeon's Promise   10
Into the Blind World Waiting   11
The Tin Man's Heart   12
Pantoum Lullaby   13
Glory Be Bop   14

Joyful   15
Advent   16
Madonna and Christ Child by Fra Angelico   17
Bananas   18
Family Picture   19
Fear Not   20
Visiting Hours   22
In the Beginning   24
Two Sparrows Sold for a Penny   25
Finding the Child   26

Luminous   27
Evolution   28
One Year Later   29
Swimming in Lake Superior   32
Harts of the Field   34
Breathing Lessons   36
Nuclear Anniversary   38

Sorrowful   39
Agony   40
Alone in a Dark Wood   41
In the Flesh   42
Dumping Ground   43

Place in the Forest   45
Low Blood Sugar   46
In the Bleak Midwinter   47
Sleeping with Grief   48

Glorious   49
Pange Lingua Gloriosi   50
For Matthew James   51
Flannery O'Connor Admiring Peacocks   52
Vase with Irises, 1890   53
Ascension on Opening Day   54
The Art of Growth   55
The Virgin's Toes   56
In the Garden   58

Biographical Note   60

The Mysteries of the Rosary

"The Religions of all Nations are derived from each Nations different reception of the Poetic Genius which is every where call'd the Spirit of Prophecy."

William Blake
"All Religions Are One"

This book is dedicated to my daughter Celeste,
the greatest mystery of my life.

Prayer

"I never felt particularly glorious at morning, noon, or evening prayer... I felt as if I were becoming part of a living, lived-in poem..."

Kathleen Norris
The Cloister Walk

Simeon's Promise

The Virgin saw the face of God
Daily, took it in her hands,
Saw Eden's requiem in His eyes.
For 33 years, she hoarded the mysteries
Of Him in her breast,
Like black pearls.
When He died, she rubbed her fingers
Raw on those dark stones, felt
The bite of His birth,
The salt of His scourging.
Did she pray on those dim gems
For the day when she would see
His face again, unfolding
Like a lightning storm,
A bright gout of love,
In the oyster of her heart?

Into the Blind World Waiting

My first communion rosary glows
Like a crow's back thick with sun.
I roll the beads with my fingers,
Pour them like oil into my palm.
The silver crucifix swims
In the puddle of black chrism,
Slick with prayers, thousands
of *Our Father*'s, *Hail Mary*'s, *Glory Be*'s.

I pray the rosary for souls
In Purgatory, a place, my mother
Whispers, that Dante got wrong,
Where angels pour molten lead
Down throats of penitent liars,
Drown regretful killers in lakes of blood,
Roast the saved selfish, like pigs on spits,
Hope riding the screams like morning fog.
My mother would drink buckets
Of quick silver rather than suffer Hell.
Hell, she says, is seeing God's face
Once, a blizzard of naked longing,
And then never again.

I pray the rosary for my sister
Whose husband left her. In her bed,
She thinks of him, their wedding day,
His hands on her skin, pressing his
Mouth to her ear, whispering words
That turn her blood into wine.
She listens for his voice now,
Four kids piled like dirty laundry
On their beds, the baby a clenched
Fist in the center of his crib,
The long seconds of night
Filled with her breath,
The memory of him
In the air like sweaty incense.

The Tin Man's Heart

The Wizard gave the Tin Man
A heart with a clock
That unwound after sundown,
Hands slowing at midnight
In the dark bed of his chest,
Each second an immense field of poppies,
Fragrant as Dorothy's thick braids.

In the forest under the stars,
The Tin Man listened to his heart tick,
Like the sound of lovers kissing,
Waiting for his spring to uncoil,
Praying for that moment:
He and Dorothy in the poppies,
The sun on their gleaming bodies.

Pantoum Lullaby

Little one, curled tight
in my love's belly,
can you hear me
sing in the night?

In my love's belly,
can you hear words I
sing in the night
as you swim and dance?

Can you hear words? I
press my hand to you
as you swim and dance
in your universe of water.

Press my hand to you,
beneath my love's heart,
in your universe of water,
dark and warm with sound.

Beneath my love's heart,
the music never ceases.
Dark and warm with sound,
you tremble and wait.

The music never ceases.
Hush little baby, I sing.
You tremble and wait
in your liquid twilight.

Hush little baby, I sing.
My voice is the moon
in your liquid twilight.
I'm calling you home.

My voice is the moon.
Can you hear me?
I'm calling you home,
Little one, curled tight.

Glory Be Bop

for Kristina, in labor
February 23, 2002

Glory be the sound of moans,
Across sky,
Black in cock-crow dawn.

Glory be the sound of blood,
Tug and wash, push and wail,
Wild midnight tide.

Glory be the sound of sweat,
Electric rain,
Hissing, kissing dark sea.

Glory be the sound of breath,
Hurricane sigh,
Hot licks on coast lips.

Glory be the sound of screams,
Seagull cry for mullet,
Wing crash, beak shred.

Glory be the sounds of you,
Bruise thick
Bright starfish on the sand.

Joyful

"Negative Capability, that is when man is capable of being in uncertainties, Mysteries, doubts, without any irritable reaching after fact and reason."

John Keats
December 21, 1817

Advent

This afternoon, a dandelion bright as a comet
blooms among brown leaves on my lawn.
A nest sits high in maple branches,
its bowl empty, hatchlings flown South.
I taste winter in the air, like incense during Mass.
My wife says she feels snow coming.

It's all about waiting and preparing, this last
month of pregnancy. I sticker nursery walls
with Winnie the Pooh and honey pots;
haul crib and changing table from the garage;
fill shelves with diapers, blankets, hand-made quilts.
Weeks ago, I painted the room gloaming purple,
a color between day and night.
My work done, I stand in the nursery's doorway,
the crib filled with November shadow.

Soon, I will bring down holiday
decorations from the attic. My wife and I will
string lights, hang ornaments, unwrap the *crèche*.
We will place Mary, Joseph, the shepherd, the angel
around the empty manger.
Tonight, I lie beside my wife, my hands on her belly.
The baby whispers against my fingertips.
Tomorrow, I will wake to snow,
feel its weight, a sleeping infant, in my arms.

Madonna and Christ Child by Fra Angelico

This December solstice, I receive
Her on a Christmas card,
A woman holding a child white as bone.
She stares at me, eyes half-open,
As she stared at Angelico six centuries ago,
Her round face smooth and vacant,
The Mediterranean on a windless night.
Her neck, slender as a piano key,
Gleams against the blue waves of her robe.
Angelico must have filled the walls of his cell
With charcoal studies of this woman's hands,
Her impossibly long fingers,
With his brushes, coaxed her lips to bloom rose,
Her chest and wide belly to blaze
Like a Florence sunrise. At matins,
He listened to doves wake
In the church eaves, slap cold night from their wings,
At vespers, tasted the grit of bread in his teeth,
Coarse and dark as crow song,
All the while thinking of her cheeks
Flushed by the work of his hands.
Maybe that is why the child looks
Almost like a man as he presses
His face to hers,
Curls his hand on her deep collar.
On Christmas Eve, Angelico closed his eyes,
Dreamed the next painted instant when
The man-child turns his lips
To her neck, dips his fingers
Even deeper on her collar,
Finds the pulse in her breast,
The rhythm of her skin.
She opens like the heavens, and his body sings
Ave to her blazing star.

Bananas

Bananas sat on my grandmother's kitchen table
Like dead sparrows turning their breasts
To the sun. They ripened to black,
Collapsing like cooling apple pies.
My grandmother caressed their skins,
Tested to see if her fingers left trails,
Paths in their withered bodies.
When they split open at the seams,
She spooned their brown jelly on toast,
Ate it with strong coffee on summer
Mornings when sun turned frosted grass
Into a galaxy of dew.

My wife freezes bananas when they blacken,
Saves them to bake loaves and muffins.
When I open the freezer door,
Dark crescents sit on the ice trays,
Hard as stone. I stroke
Their slick curves, imagine the meat
Within waiting to soften, burst open,
Seep into the air like a lost aurora borealis
Over Hunama Bay, in Hawaii,
Where I'm sitting on a shoal of coral,
Eating pineapple. The ocean has salted my lips.

My 6-month-old daughter calls
From the living room. Her mouth is filled
With a fluorescent donut.
Taste is her key, as if she could
Read the Braille of the universe
With her tongue. If I give her a frozen banana,
I wonder what mysteries she would unlock,
If she would taste the sun trapped in its sweet eclipse,
The cold of my grandmother's fingertips,
The dark nut of bread, the oil jelly
Waves of the Pacific blinding the white reef.

Family Picture

All of us together for the first time in about ten years and the cameras crack like machine guns and people yell, "Wait, just one more!" as my nine-month-old daughter screams in my wife's arms, wanting DOWN and AWAY, insistent, and my wife paces back-and-forth because we've been waiting all day for everybody to be here, Fred from L.A., Kevin from across town, Paul from Iron Mountain, Mary from her five kids, on and on: Fred's new wife Diane, blonde and loud with laughter, herself an only child, glows in this roomful of family, family, family—so much family that the windows are sweating with breath and everyone is itching for the Pizza Hut guy to show up to feed us, so hungry from being together we could eat each other.

Fear Not

My sister Rose spoke with the Virgin
One night when lightning laced
The sky and thunder rolled
Like a wailing ambulance.
Rose, with black hair, eyes dark
As baker's chocolate. Rose, who listened
To the rain drill the ground, felt terror
In her chest, blooming like a mushroom.
Rose, with Down's Syndrome,
Her speech thick,
Weighing on her tongue like rust.

She knew nothing of atmospheres,
Weather fronts, lightning that traveled
From the ground to the heavens
Like a white hot soul. She knew
Nothing of raining frogs,
Hailstones the size of peach pits.
Hers was a child's fear, as simple
As shadow in a closet.
When she knelt at the foot of her bed,
Folded small fingers,
Her prayers opened like sunflowers
In the still air.

Mother found Rose that night,
Speaking with the darkness.
She looked like moonlight, her words
Agates, smooth, round, polished.
Rose, imperfect since birth,
Slower than summer heat,
Filled the room with light.

Anne came upon her daughter
Like that, too, Mary in the dark,
Her childhood fears sitting
On the windowsill like empty bowls
Waiting for rain.

Mary spread her arms,
Wrapped them around the angel,
Pressing her mouth to his neck.
She tasted lightning and shadow
On his bright skin, swallowed them,
Felt them take root
In her belly. She opened
Her robe, guided his lips
To her boy chest,
Motherhood swelling
In her rose nipple.

Visiting Hours

I.

My wife spends the weekend sitting
beside her uncle's bed,
watching him shrink beneath the sheet,
draw inward like witch hazel touched
by October frost. His brain is mapped
by blood, by a clot that roared
through his head like some dark star.
I wonder if he felt its approach,
knew it was coming, the way
astronomers know Halley's Comet
returns every seventy-six years.
And when it appears in the sky,
blazing ice and fire,
people drive to midnight shores,
away from the glow of city,
to see it, a bullet of light,
frozen above the sand and surf.

II.

He doesn't flinch.
His eyes don't roam his eyelids for dreams.
My wife talks to him, about cranberry bars
and our one-year-old's fall down
a flight of stairs. She holds his hand,
and when she leaves, presses her lips
against his cool forehead, imagines him
in the cave of his skull, feeling
her touch, eating her whispered words.
His chest rises. Falls. Rises. Falls.
Each breath an eclipse in the white room.

III.

My wife has not seen him for three days now.
She calls for updates, reports
of altered breaths and hand movements.
When she sleeps at night, she sees him
in his dim universe, a fetus,
sucking his fist, running his wordless
tongue over knuckles and fingers.
No miracle is coming. No star
to lead him over scorched earth,
through wind and canyon,
to warm dung and fresh hay.
He waits for the final word,
the last touch, the kiss
to launch him into orbit.

In the Beginning

Celeste rolls on the carpet
like dice that won't pause
on green felt, won't give
me the satisfaction
of 3 or 6, 1 or 5.
There is too much in her
knee-and-wall world to touch, too
many snakes with cardboard wings,
neon troikas plastered with words—
apple, *cow*, *star*. When I speak to her,
she studies me, tries to unravel
my dictionary of sound.
Can I teach her to love language
the way lightning loves redwoods?
What will her first word be?
Will she shock me
with *hamster, fridge, triangle*? Will
she point out the window, say
wind? Will she sing the world,
the way Christ sang when He slid
from Mary's iron-taut uterus,
tasted her blood, saw Joseph radiant
with sweat? Will Celeste's mouth open,
flood waters pour out, 40 days
and nights, preparing the world
for the rainbow of her tongue?

Two Sparrows Sold for a Penny

My daughter hands me
the wing of a bird,
ragged, stripped almost to the bone
of feathers. I hold the wing,
its shoulder joint oily with blood.
My daughter smiles, claps
as if she has just given me
a piece of toast or a raisin,
her face bright as sea foam.

I picture a crippled sparrow
panting in deep grass, a cat
licking its claws clean, an owl
lining its nest with skull and spine.
I want to drop my daughter's gift,
urge her to see
the cleaving of the body,
decay, hunger, the fear
of sudden shadow.

I hold the wing, cupped
in my palm like precious water,
and, in my daughter's face,
see clouds and blue sky,
the sun gleaming on the distant
arrow of a bird
in the heavens.

Finding the Child

for Danielle van Dam (1994 - 2002)

She must have looked like bleached
Driftwood when they found her
In the desert, her hair a halo of sand,
Her eyes blanched with sun.
I imagine her last dawn, an O'Keefe
Landscape, pink and white and bone.
Did she gaze skyward, her heart,
A mariposa lily in her thin chest,
Unfurling, breathing the coming day?
Did she lift her hands to the heavens,
The way a daughter reaches
For her father when she wakes?
Did she hear the rattlesnake coil
Under the stone, its jaws
Gentle as a midnight comet,
Its tail, distant rain?
Did she taste dry cactus spine
In the bud of her mouth,
Her breath sharp with blood?
Did the air settle on her
Like warm adobe?
Did she wrap her arms around
The neck of the daystar and lift herself
To the milky breast of morning?

Luminous

"To feel the love of people whom we
love is a fire that feeds our life..."

Pablo Neruda

"I am someone who proudly and humbly affirms
that love is the mystery-of-mysteries..."

e. e. cummings

Evolution

Miss Hale was an experiment for Assumption Grotto School.
In her not-quite-miniskirts and thigh-high boots,
She was Technicolor while the nuns were black-and-white.
Marching into my sixth grade, Miss Hale's heels
Sparked lightning from the tile. Her hair was black
As a confessional; eyes, brown as Saint Francis.
I swallowed every word she spoke,
Felt them living inside me so that at night,
She was my prayer I lifted to God:
Hale Mary, full of grace and
Our Father, who art in heaven, Hale be thy name.

One day, Miss Hale told us,
"I'm going to teach you where we all come from."
I hunkered down, expecting her to say
Words that burned my tongue.
She produced maps of Africa,
Spoke of origins and Darwin and Galapagos,
Described Louis Leakey and missing links and ancestor apes.
As her last piece of evidence, she turned her back to us,
Pressed her hand at the base of her spine, and said,
"Here's where our tails used to be."

That night, I dreamed I had a tail, thick and wild.
I cracked coconuts with my teeth, sucked the milk,
Let it spill white down my arms, chest, thighs.
Miss Hale, hair blinding black in the jungle sun,
Sat high in a tree, her tail snaking the air,
Inviting me to climb. I climbed,
And our chimpanzee screams shook the vines like rain.

One Year Later

for Beth
October 14, 1996

1. Driving along the lake

Girders of light support an autumn sun
against the underbelly of the sky. Lake
Michigan, white gold to the horizon,
continues its Ice Age mission: waves
grinding stones to sand, sand washing
into beaches, beaches growing and shrinking
with the rising and falling moon. Wind
rucks the lake's surface, air set in motion
by some cosmic magnetism.

But seagulls bobbing in the cold waters
know nothing of tides, winds, the cosmos.
They pound their wings against the dusk,
gulp mouthfuls of liquid gold,
and scream for fish.

2. At the foot of the cross

Some people climb the 29 marble steps
on their knees, saying a prayer for each
step Christ climbed to stand before Pilate.
I have never done it, but I wonder
if the stone would feel like thorns
biting into my shins. We look up at
the goal of our pilgrimage: the world's
largest crucifix, the sign on I-75 proclaims.
The face stares down at us
from the 150-foot-redwood cross,
and I contemplate all the guilt
and sin wound into this figure
of bronze agony.

Gazing up at its dark curves, I grow
dizzy watching clouds scud across the sky.
Suddenly the whole world is moving,
sky rotating, trees bowing, sun spinning.
The cross sways, Christ writhing against
His spikes. A moment of vertigo,
a moment when the entire universe whirlpools
around my unbalanced senses as if the finger
of God has touched me, made me the center
of creation. Beside me, you kneel, whisper to Him.
The sun fires white gold on your cheeks.

3. Scaffolding work

My grandmother once told me
nobody ever saw baby pigeons. I imagined
purple sand and black water, a shore
squirming with pink hatchlings hungry
to sprout feathers and invade
the gutters and rooftops of the world.

Working on rotting eaves, three stories
of scaffolding shifting beneath my step,
I curse pigeons. I pry planks loose.
Mounds of dirt, feathers, wood,
shit shower on my upturned face.
I drive home new boards, feel nails
sinking into soft support beams.
I wonder how long the repairs will last,
splints holding together limbs
that should be amputated. I wonder
if the builders thought pigeons would
shatter an upstairs window one winter,
claw into the rafters, and freeze
to death, beating their wings bloody
against the attic floor.

The nest sits on the last board,
a mound of mud, grass, feathers.
A fat pigeon swoops from the corner,

slaps at my cheeks until they burn.
I bat the bird away, breathless.
A pink head appears above the nest's lip.
A sound breaks from its beak,
the sound a dying butterfly would make.
I consider tearing the board away,
watching the creature bounce off brick,
plummet to cement, explode like a water balloon.
A cold wind fills the bowl of the nest.
The hatchling struggles over the brim,
dangles from a stray twig
for a moment, and then falls,
skidding against the eighty-year-old building,
sparking blood. It turns white gold,
a meteor burning to dust in the atmosphere.

4. October 14

A friend reads this unfinished poem,
asks what pigeons, tides, crosses have
to do with anniversaries. I don't know.
I stare at the white gold you placed
on my finger a year ago. I think of
everything I want to understand,
like the pull of the moon, the pain
of faith, the need to fly. Even though I
know why Lake Michigan crawls in and out,
I scream at the sky. Even though I have read
the gospels, I burn my eyes in the sun.
Even though the scaffolding is steady, I jump.
When I sleep with you, feel the curve
of your breast in my hand, the heat of your
back against my stomach, I understand you.
Yet, in the night, listening to the drum
of your heart, I watch your eyes
move beneath your lids.
You dream and shimmer and glow.
A mystery.

Swimming in Lake Superior

for Kristina in Washington

1. Salt

I have swum in the Pacific,
In a bay so blue the sky was white.
I chased parrot fish, like blue
Green breaths, through salt.
A freshwater swimmer, I gulped
A mouthful of brine, expecting quench
And sun, a swallow that washes
Ham sandwich to your stomach.
The water burned my lips and gums,
Made my teeth bleed.

In the hotel room two hours later,
I still tasted the ocean.
My tongue was a jellyfish,
Gliding along the curve of my wife's spine,
Seeking her pools of dark salt,
The rush of surf, the bite of coral.

2. Winter

I hear Lake Superior is warm
This summer. You can swim its shoreline,
And the cold doesn't squeeze lungs,
Cripple ankles. I am suspicious.
I remember plunging into the lake,
Treading and kicking, sweating snow.
Hours later, when I hold my lips
Against my arm, I feel my skin melt,
Icicle gleaming wet in sunlight.
Like salt in the Pacific, I expect
Superior to be saturated with winter.
After swimming, I expect my body
To be a blizzard, a blinding ache.

But, this August, Superior is warm.
I cannot feel that December touch.
I think of you at the Pacific,
Diving into the August surf, lips pressed
Together to fight off the taste of tears.

Harts of the Field

Wild apple steeps the clearing,
Sweet and ripe on the green carpet
Of needles. The waxwing twists
Her head so her beak, thin and brown,
Strokes the cold air. She swallows
A piece of apple. It bobs
In her throat, a buoy in rough water.
Her gold-dust feathers flash.
She trills. Her voice hangs
In the spruces like ice.
I watch her stretch her wings,
Like a lover in early light.
She rises into the sky, brushing
The morning with music.

A squirrel with fur the color of smoke
Stares at me. In the black mirrors of her eyes,
I see myself, an Easter Island statue,
Shadow and silence, eclipsing her need
For acorn. I smell smoke from a neighbor's
Chimney, clean laundry, fallen leaves
Slick with snow melt. The squirrel
Waits, tail still, in the blue afternoon.
A cloud blots the sun. She flinches,
Flattens herself against the earth,
As if the sudden darkness weighs
On her back like a hawk's claw.
Then, she arcs away from me, over
The fresh snow, moving like a stone
Skipped across the surface of a lake.

On the breast of the hill, a doe
Bends her slender neck
To tall grass, her slow tongue tasting
The frost of dusk. Her breath mists
The air, rises to the quarter moon
Already bright in the sky. Her ears
Quiver, alert for the approach of skunk,

Black bear, or buck. I watch her
On the ridge, the curve of her back,
The muscle of her legs. She moves
With the night, following it
Down the hill, into the bed of the forest.

Breathing Lessons

I had a picnic the day my grandmother died.
Her death was no surprise.
All week long, I'd been hearing
About her breathing. Monday, my mother
Told me, "She's breathing like a train
Going uphill." "Like crickets,"
My sister said on Wednesday.
"Like crickets in the night."
When I went to see her on Thursday,
She was on oxygen. The tube under
Her nose hissed with air
She wasn't using. Each breath
Hit her like a hammer.
She looked deflated, a balloon swan
Two days after a carnival. I stood
By her bed, watching her lungs limp
Through the seconds. *Like a trout,*
I thought. *Like a trout on an August beach.*

She died on Saturday morning.
My father recited the rosary by her side.
I was in my basement office at school
with my girlfriend, drinking merlot.
We fed each other strawberries
Dipped in chocolate. We ate by candlelight,
Two tall candles dripping purple
Wax on the desk. I unbuttoned her shirt,
Saw the pearl of her shoulder glowing
In the flickering shadow.
I ran my fingers through her hair,
Pressed my lips to her nipple, and heard
Her breath stop.
My hands moved down her back,
Between her legs, and coaxed the air
From her body again, short and rapid,
Then longer and deeper. I watched her
Close her eyes, listened to her breathe,
As easy as sunlight. I could smell

Chocolate when she exhaled.
I pressed my ear to her chest,
Heard a train going uphill,
Crickets in the night,
A trout on an August beach.

Nuclear Anniversary

Wedding cake thawed after 50 years
tastes like freezer, venison,
and popsicle. White curls
around the dark meat and a rose
as purple as *The Sower* waits
for the quiet apocalypse of lips.

Sugar undergoes a radioactive shift,
from grains to chocolate to ice
to this chimera, at once frost and frosting,
the physics of marriage.
It's all about orbits and attractions,
bodies at rest and in motion.
The man and woman collide on their wedding night,
like uranium particles over the Bikinis.
Their atoms spin and spark
into constellation, a winter so bright
the snow glows at midnight.

At solstice, long icicle of dusk,
that first fusion of man and woman
becomes thick nickel in the eye,
a gray place where he lights a candle,
she spreads bedding on the concrete.
They open canned fruit, and she thinks
of a lover as gold as peach slices,
he of a daughter buried under an apple tree.
The man reaches for the woman,
touches her rice paper skin, feels
her flicker beneath his fingers.

They sit, slice bites of wedding cake,
And feed them to each other.

Sorrowful

"Were it possible for us to see further than our knowledge reaches... perhaps we would endure our sadnesses with greater confidence than our joys."

Rainer Maria Rilke
Letters To A Young Poet

"I have it in me so much nearer home
To scare myself with my own desert places."

Robert Frost
"Desert Places"

Agony

I have seen a testicle swimming
in a bottle like a forgotten olive,
round and veined and milky, waiting
to be labeled, examined, and incinerated,
like foreskin trimmed from a wailing infant,
like the black stump of an umbilical
cord, that rope of nourishment
so necessary *in utero*,
remnant of another universe of water.

That bottled testicle,
sitting on a table draped in cloth,
makes me ponder
my knee throbbing for rain,
a silver hair from my temple,
my body's decline and disintegration,
its fragmentation and return
to clay, not incorruptible
like Saint Theresa, who still gives off
the scent of roses after a century
in the tomb, not a fleshy miracle,
like the foreskin of Christ, guarded
by monks in a medieval monastery,
healing the lame and unpossessing
the possessed—no, my body,
my taste of agony
in a garden of sleeping fools.

Alone in a Dark Wood

The night roosts like a murder
Of crows in the November jack pines.
I stare into moonless void.
In the bracken, something watches.
I feel its eyes on my face,
Imagine it crouched in the grass,
Chuffing frost. If I lunge, I could
Crush it against my chest. If I stand still,
It could disappear in the midnight fog.
I hear movement, like the whisper of ant legs,
A slender, black icicle of sound. I listen
For more, a car or the wind or the whine
Of a bear cub. Where is Virgil to guide me
Away from the dark gaze
Of this skunk or fox or she-wolf?
Where is his dim hand to hold,
His voice, distant as the stars,
Commanding, "Follow," leading
Through this wood where Beatrice
Has abandoned me, alone and wounded?
I listen again. An owl wails.
A rabbit darts to dirt and roots.

In the Flesh

The first time I held birth,
It lay in my palm
Looking like an amputated pinky.
A baby of my sister's gerbil, it burned
My hand and breathed
Six breaths to every one of mine.
Its tail, instead of being straight,
Was crimped at an angle.
Hind legs, atrophied,
Hung like threads of skin
Snagged from its body.
It wriggled about with its litter mates,
Eyes sealed by birth like theirs,
But never to open, never to be startled
By light. Nursed from an eye dropper,
It grew downy brown, yet
Its tail remained crooked; legs, withered;
Eyes, shut and rimmed with discharge
Dried the color of blood.
On the morning it died, I reached
Into the cage, lifted it from the cedar.
For a moment, I mistook
Its cold for warmth, the way an ice cube
First burns the touch.

Dumping Ground

Like some drunk Homer, Brian
Talks of the Dumping Ground,
A place in the middle of the woods
Where the bodies are piled to treetops,
Skunks and raccoons, porcupines and deer,
Victims of the asphalt,
Stacked and sorted like laundry.
Brian says clouds of flies eclipse
The sun, tear the air like sirens.
The smell, stiff with blood and fur,
Passes through the trees like wind,
Stirs pine needles, and makes birds
Dive for worms not there.

When Brian stops speaking,
The night, dark as the inside of a skull,
Almost makes me believe his story.
I close my eyes, see a doe chasing
Her fawn away from the morning commute.
She smells coffee in the cab of the Dodge
That shreds her pupils with windshield.
A skunk scents Whopper wrappers
Along U.S. 41. He tastes perch and lake
In his last breath. A raccoon watches her mate
Test the black ribbon of Dead River Road.
She waits for him to rise until dawn.

How do these fallen creatures end up
In the Dumping Ground? Scraped or shoveled
Into orange county trucks and flung
Onto heaps in the forest?
Or carried on the backs of moose,
A procession attended by mole and crow,
Snapping turtle and beaver, moving
Through the trees, bearing the bodies
To wild Golgotha.

There, under the stars, the dead wait.
A deer's legs reach for Virgo,

Paw the heavens for blueberries
And sweet, green grass. Her ribs,
White as cloud, cage the dark,
Hold the secrets of mosquito and grub.
A black bear stands at the clearing's edge,
Hungry, his muzzle buried in the moon,
And groans for crabapples and midnight moss,
The hollow cave of deep winter.

Place in the Forest

With one B-B, Paul took the squirrel down.
When it hit the ground, it screamed
A squirrel scream, high and long
Like a train whistle raised five octaves.
It scratched the earth
Like it was trying to dig its own grave,
A bead of blood flowering on its back.
Paul and I watched it spasm and slow,
A wind-up toy uncoiling its tense spring.
It raced breaths in-out-in-out-in-out-in-out.

In school, we read about Vlad the Impaler
Who feasted on roasted pig in a field of people
On spikes. The wood-cut illustration showed
Vlad sipping wine from a chalice
As a pregnant woman slithered down
A pointed pole, her mouth a black leech of pain.
Paul found a stick, skewered the squirrel,
Which writhed, scratched at the bark.
He lifted the stick, raised the squirrel
To the sky. Its tail snaked and batted
The clouds. Paul flung the squirrel
Into the woods, its scream cleaving the air.

Ten years later, he died of AIDS.
I thought of that squirrel when I heard
Stories of the red sarcoma blossoms
On his face. I imagined him
In his hospital bed, his chest heaving,
His eyes seeing that place in the forest
Where squirrels wail and claw.

Low Blood Sugar

for Penny

Sitting down for Thanksgiving dinner,
My father always says the same thing:
"I could eat the asshole of a skunk raw."
He fasts all day, saving room for turkey and pie,
But he doesn't know real hunger,
Low-blood-sugar hunger. He doesn't understand
When I talk about hunger so deep
I could gnaw my arm down to bone, suck
The marrow like a teenage boy's first sex,
Hot and quick and devouring.

Imagine a thirst so thick your tongue
Swells the size of a watermelon
You can't slice open, pink meat
You can't caress in your mouth.
Imagine waking up next to your lover
At midnight, wanting to touch her
As she moans your name in her sleep.
Now imagine you have no hands.

Penny knows low blood sugar.
Last week, as she drove home,
Her pickup spun. She watched
Earth become heaven.
Heaven become earth.
She didn't feel her leg splinter,
Teeth break, tongue mushroom blood.
She knew only longing,
The hungry darkness coming,
Reaching out, like a handless lover.

In the Bleak Midwinter

In the Ishpeming cemetery, a statue
of the Virgin Mary stands over
the grave of a nine-year-old boy.
My mother once told me myrrh
was a spice used in death,
that Mary knew her baby would die.
In the dark, the statue glows
like carved moonlight.
The first time I saw the Virgin at night,
I looked up, into her face, her forehead
smooth as ice, her eyes white and liquid,
her cheeks, stained
as if she had been crying blood.
This holiday season, I work my fingers
raw making wreaths. Winding and pulling,
I feel the string digging into the creases
of my knuckles. Sap stains my skin black,
and for days, I cannot make a fist
without my hands splitting open,
my blood smelling like cedar.

Tonight, snow is falling
on the ground like notes from a flute,
wavering and delicate. The Virgin
shines, catches flakes in the palms
of her outstretched hands.
A Christmas wreath rests on the grave
before her—its ribbon bears two words
in gold: "Beloved Son."
I imagine the boy's mother kneeling
at Mary's feet, placing the wreath
the way the Magi placed the myrrh,
her heart swelling with sorrow.

Sleeping with Grief

I don't know what to do with my wife's grief,
How she clutches my shirt,
Weeps the way Eve wept for Abel,
Sorrow wild, thick as locusts.

She says grief sits in her stomach,
Fills her up like Thanksgiving dinner.
I imagine carving grief, serving it
With stuffing, black and full of onion.

I'm trying to understand
How despair works, how being alone
Is like burying her mother again.

I'm not alone, she says.
When you leave, grief crawls
Into bed with me. I can't say no.
I can't close my eyes, turn my back.

At night, in the dark, I lie
Next to my wife, put my arm across
Her sleeping body, feel her chest
Rise and fall, slow as a funeral.

If I press my ear to her breast,
I will hear the sound Eve made
When God introduced her to death.

Glorious

"The world is charged with the grandeur of God…"

Gerard Manley Hopkins
"God's Grandeur"

Pange Lingua Gloriosi
("Sing My Tongue the Savior's Glory")

On Holy Saturday, I put my daughter
To sleep and think of death.
Tonight, milk is her enemy.
She stands in her crib, dark eyes watering,
Her chin slick with fear. I lift her,
Strip off her wet pajamas, wash her fevered body
With a cold cloth. She shivers, yet lies still,
Accepting the bath in silence. I dress her,
Fresh and lotioned, place her back inside the crib
My wife has just cleaned, cover her with a quilt,
And watch her settle into the pillows
Like a sleeping fish.

Before Easter, these quiet moments
In the dark, there is this:
I listen to my daughter's breaths,
As Mary might have listened to her son's,
Counting them
Like stars in the night.

For Matthew James

born February 15, 1995

He's celebrating his zero birthday in an incubator, not moving, trying to give himself the present of a breath. From the moment I found out he existed, I called him tadpole. That was before I knew his sex, when all I pictured was the collision of egg and sperm, the wild instant of beginning. For nine months, I imagined some amphibian man, a creature from the womb-lagoon, able to breathe fluid. This morning, when the doctor split his heaven open with a scalpel and reached down to deliver him, he gulped one last liquid breath. "It happens all the time," the pediatrician tells his father and mother, "Nothing to worry about." In this world of air, he is a netted fish, a mer-baby threatened by the foam in his lungs. We stand by the nursery window, watch a nurse come in and touch him. He quivers, his legs bent in a birth *plié*. His chest rises, falls, stops. Rises. Stops. Falls. Stops. The nurse withdraws her hands. He begins to remember his lungs again, remembers the measured bites of air, the occupation of breathing: his life-long inheritance.

Flannery O'Connor Admiring Peacocks

(Inspired by her essay "The King of the Birds")

I want to strut and shiver myself into full bloom
So the Bible salesman coming down the road
Will look at me and cry out, "Jesus! Risen Jesus!"
Like he's at a Pentecostal tent revival.

I want to gorge myself on chrysanthemums and roses
Until petals carpet the Georgia clay,
Rain transforms the petals into pools
Of gold and red tears.

I want to roost in the oak trees, and at midnight,
Open my throat, scream for the absent sun,
For the darkness riding in my tail,
Deep and heavy like a tombstone.

I want to stop the farmhand in his tracks,
At dawn, when he sees me perched
On top of the barn, blazing
Like stained glass on Easter morning.

I want to feel my train
Lifting behind me, unfolding
Horizons of green-bronze souls,
A *galaxy of gazing, haloed suns.*

Vase with Irises, 1890

The blossoms, a swarm
of wrecked hummingbirds, blue,
crumpled, try to escape
the gold fist of the vase.
The static of wings beats
the saffron sunlight to a froth.
Needle beaks stab and stab
the fronds curving away like green fire.

How long did this arrangement last?
How long did the universe spin
above this hungry star? Imagine
van Gogh trying to contain
this unruly host, already rebelling,
questioning the power of brush and paint.
Imagine his white hot mind
holding the scene together,
flinging these blue angels, one-by-one,
into the eternity of his canvas.

Ascension on Opening Day

In the tangle of bracken
Out back, a spikehorn leaps
Three times,

Then plows to the ground,
Horsehoeing the trunk of a poplar
With its yearling antlers.

Its ears shudder
As if vexed by the deerflies of summer.
Breath fogs its muzzle.

The wound in its neck,
Round as the head of a nail,
Steams with blood.

It blinks
At the bright floor of the heavens,
Sees clouds, white like forest.

It paws the snow to black dirt,
Kicks and bucks, as if running
Up the hill,

Through the slalom of birches,
To a haven of jack pine,
Moss, and swamp.

The Art of Growth

A coworker carries her granddaughter
around the office, showing off
her dark curls and serious eyes.
I am amazed how much the child
has grown, size her up
like a blue-ribbon squash.
The last time I saw her,
she fit into the fold of my arm,
a mitten of sleep. Now,
in this thick June, she is
all height and weight, a moving
field of sprout and fruit.

My coworker knows the art of growth,
the moisture and heat it needs,
the cycles of sowing and reaping.
With her daughter, she kneads manure
into black earth, thick with cow smell,
watches her granddaughter plow
dirt with her fingers.
I wonder if she is ever astonished
by the size of her roses,
the yellow of her daylilies.
I wonder if she ever listens
to her garden at night,
the way I listen to my daughter
stretch and grow in the dark.

The Virgin's Toes

The Virgin stares through bulletproof glass
from her ledge in the grotto.
I used to be able to touch her
when I was a child. I could boost myself
onto the marble altar at her feet,
reach up, run my fingers over her toes.
When I told the priest this in confession,
he asked what her toes felt like.
"Like toes," I told him because I didn't yet have
the experience of my dead grandmother's cold knuckles.

Covering the walls of the grotto are hooks,
sometimes punctuating the inscriptions
chiseled in the donated bricks
like three-dimensional question marks:
IN LOVING MEMORY?
My mother said it's just like Lourdes,
where crippled pilgrims come aided
by canes or crutches,
worship at the Virgin's feet,
hang their canes or crutches
on the wall and walk away.

I never saw anything hanging
from the hooks at Assumption Grotto,
although Sister Bernadette told
our third grade class about a little girl
with cerebral palsy who was carried
to the grotto on a stretcher, twisted and twitching,
and while her parents prayed,
stood up and began singing Schubert's *Ave Maria*,
in the angel Gabriel's voice, Sister said,
trying to inspire us. At recess that day,
we watched the grotto at the back of the cemetery,
listening for angels over the traffic of Gratiot Avenue.
"Isn't that a shame?" my aunt says, nodding
at the bulletproof glass, installed after
some pilgrim used the Virgin for target practice.

Her words echo in the half shell of the grotto.
"Why would anybody want to do that?"
She crosses herself.
I gaze at the Virgin's feet,
at the miracle of the Virgin's toes,
at the grotto's empty hooks.

In the Garden

I can put my fist in the hole
in my sister's flank, see rib
white against slick muscle.
When she sleeps, her body cries
for healthy blood and skin and scar.
I sit beside her hospital bed, listen
to her breaths, wonder if she dreams
of dog bites, sharp glass,
the thick kiss of a dead love.
The man down the hall moans
"Clara" in the dark,
a two-syllable prayer
for deep winter, pine cones,
cool fingers on his naked back.
My sister's hand flutters on the sheet.
I touch her wrist, trace the blue veins
under the skin. Her face smoothes
like a snowdrift, and I see
the pulse leap in her temple,
nostrils black with air,
eyes vagrant beneath their lids.

Her wound has not healed for two years,
and I joke she has stigmata like Padre Pio,
beg her to touch my head, bless me.
She laughs, crosses the air.
When the priest visits her, my sister says,
"I feel like someone forgot to bury me."
He anoints her forehead, hands, and feet.
During her next dressing change,
my sister grips the rails of the bed,
bites her lip until it bruises, splits.
The nurse examines the discharge,
smells the wound for infection, then leaves.
My sister cradles her stomach, as if afraid
her heart may spill onto the floor.

Pio's wounds smelled of violets,
the petals of his fingers raising
full-moon hosts to heaven
during mass, roses blooming
on the snow of his bandages.
He bled all day, enough to fill
a chalice to its golden lip.
For five decades, he nursed
the stigmata like fragile orchids
rooted in his body's soil.
At night, in his cell, he stripped
his dressings, allowed his suffering
to breathe the dark air, nerve endings
sparking in his ragged skin
like fireflies in tall grass.
In the few hours he slept,
his body opened, unfurled
the deep ovule of his pain
until the floor, walls, ceiling
blossomed with his bruised fragrance.

Tonight, my sister rests.
The IV fills her, the way rain fills
a summer garden. She holds
her side, blooms in her bed,
a fresh and open miracle.

Biographical Note

Martin Achatz is an adjunct instructor of English at Northern Michigan University, where he received his MA in fiction and MFA in poetry. His work has appeared in *Kenesaw Review* and *Paterson Literary Review*. He lives with his wife, Beth, and their three-year-old daughter, Celeste, in the Upper Peninsula of Michigan, not far from the shores of Lake Superior.

Other books from Mayapple Press

John Repp, *White Doe,* 2004
    Paper, 40 pp, $8.50 plus s&h
    ISBN 0-932412-27-0
Dennis Hinrichsen, *Message to Be Spoken into the Left Ear of God,* 2004
    Paper, 52 pp, $8.50 plus s&h
    ISBN 0-932412-26-2
Johnny Durán, *Nieblas de Luna / Moon Fogs,* 2004
    Paper, 52 pp, $8.50 plus s&h
    ISBN 0-932412-23-8
Adrienne Lewis, *Coming Clean,* 2003
    Paper, 30 pp, $8 plus s&h
    ISBN 0-932412-21-1
Pamela Miller, *Recipe for Disaster,* 2003
    Paper, 66 pp, $12 plus s&h
    ISBN 0-932412-19-X
Gerry LaFemina, *Zarathustra in Love,* 2001
    Paper, 44 pp, $8.50 plus s&h
    ISBN 0-932412-18-1
Judith Kerman and Don Riggs, eds.,
Uncommonplaces: Poems of the Fantastic, 2000
    Paper, 148 pp, $15 plus s&h
    ISBN 0-932412-17-3
Poems by leading s.f. and fantasy authors, including Brian Aldiss, Joe Haldeman, Jeanne Larsen, David Lunde, Patrick O'Leary, Rick Wilber, & Jane Yolen
Helen Ruggieri, *Glimmer Girls,* 1999
    Paper, 40 pp, $8 plus s&h
    ISBN 0-932412-16-5
Zack Rogow, *The Selfsame Planet,* 1999
    Paper, 40 pp, $7.50 plus s&h
    ISBN 0-932412-15-7
Larry Levy, *I Would Stay Forever If I Could,* 1999
    Paper, 36 pp, $6.50 plus s&h
    ISBN 0-932412-14-9
Skip Renker, *Sifting the Visible,* 1998
    Paper, 36 pp, $6.50 plus s&h
    ISBN 0-932412-13-0
Hugh Fox, *Strata,* 1998
    Paper, 28 pp, $5.50 plus s&h
    ISBN 0-932412-12-2
John Palen, *Staying Intact,* 1997
    Paper, 28 pp, $6 plus s&h
    ISBN 0-932412-11-4

Judith McCombs, *Territories, Here & Elsewhere,* 1996
  Paper, 28 pp, $6 plus s&h
  ISBN 0-932412-10-6
Kip Zegers, *The American Floor,* 1996
  Paper, 24 pp, $6 plus s&h
  ISBN 0-932412-09-2
Al Hellus, *a vision of corrected history with breakfast,* 1995
  Paper, 24 pp, $5 plus s&h
  ISBN 0-932412-08-4
David Lunde, *Blues for Port City,* 1995
  Paper, 24 pp, $5 plus s&h
  ISBN 0-932412-07-8
Evelyn Wexler, *Occupied Territory,* 1994
  Paper, 80 pp, $10 plus s&h
  ISBN 0-932412-06-8
Evelyn Wexler, *The Geisha House,* 1992
  Paper, 24 pp, $5.50 plus s&h
  ISBN 0-932412-05-X
Judith Minty, *Letters to my Daughters,* 1981
  Paper, 24 pp, $5 plus s&h
  ISBN 0-932412-04-3
Toni Ortner-Zimmerman, *As If Anything Could Grow Back Perfect,* 1979
  Paper, 16 pp, $5 plus s&h
  ISBN 0-932412-02-5

Also available through Mayapple Press:
Judith Kerman, *Plane Surfaces / Plano de Incidencia,* 2002, CCLEH
  Bilingual, translations by Johnny Durán
  Paper, 144 pp, $15 plus s&h
  ISBN 0-932412-20-3
Dulce María Loynaz, *La Carta de Amor al Rey Tut-Ank-Amen /*
The Love Letter to King Tutankhamen, 2002, CCLEH
  Bilingual, translation by Judith Kerman.
  Limited edition of 250, signed & numbered.
  Paper, 28 pp, $10 plus s&h
  ISBN 0-932412-24-6
Judith Kerman, *Mothering & Dream of Rain,* 1996, Ridgeway Press
  Paper, 88 pp, $12 plus s&h
  ISBN 0-932412-22-X
Judith Kerman, *3 Marbles,* 1999, Cranberry Tree
  Paper, 32 pp, $7 plus s&h
  ISBN 0-9684218-1-4
Judith Kerman, *Driving for Yellow Cab,* 1985, Tout Press
  Paper, 16 pp, $5 plus s&h
  ISBN 0-932412-04-1

Sample poems and the latest information for all Mayapple Press publications are available online at ***www.mayapplepress.com***

www.ingramcontent.com/pod-product-compliance
Lightning Source LLC
Chambersburg PA
CBHW072112290426
44110CB00014B/1892